MANFISH

A Story of Jacques Cousteau

by Jennifer Berne

illustrated by
Éric Puybaret

chronicle books · san francisco

BUBBLES RISING
THROUGH THE SILENCE OF THE SEA,
SILVERY BEADS OF BREATH
FROM A MAN
DEEP, DEEP DOWN
IN A STRANGE AND SHIMMERING OCEAN LAND
OF SWAYING PLANTS AND FANTASTIC CREATURES,
A MANFISH
SWIMMING, DIVING
INTO THE UNKNOWN,
EXPLORING UNDERWATER WORLDS

NO ONE HAD EVER SEEN

AND NO ONE COULD EVER HAVE IMAGINED.

OUR STORY starts many years before, in France, with a little baby boy born under the summer sun.

His parents named him Jacques.

From the very beginning little Jacques loved water—the way it felt on his hands, his face, his body. And water made him wonder. He wondered why ships floated. Why he floated. And why rocks sank.

One day Jacques read a story about a man who hid underwater by breathing through a long tube. Jacques tried it and discovered it was impossible.

He dreamed that someday he would be able to breathe underwater for real.

At night Jacques dreamed he could fly. With the birds, among the clouds, with his arms stretched out like wings.

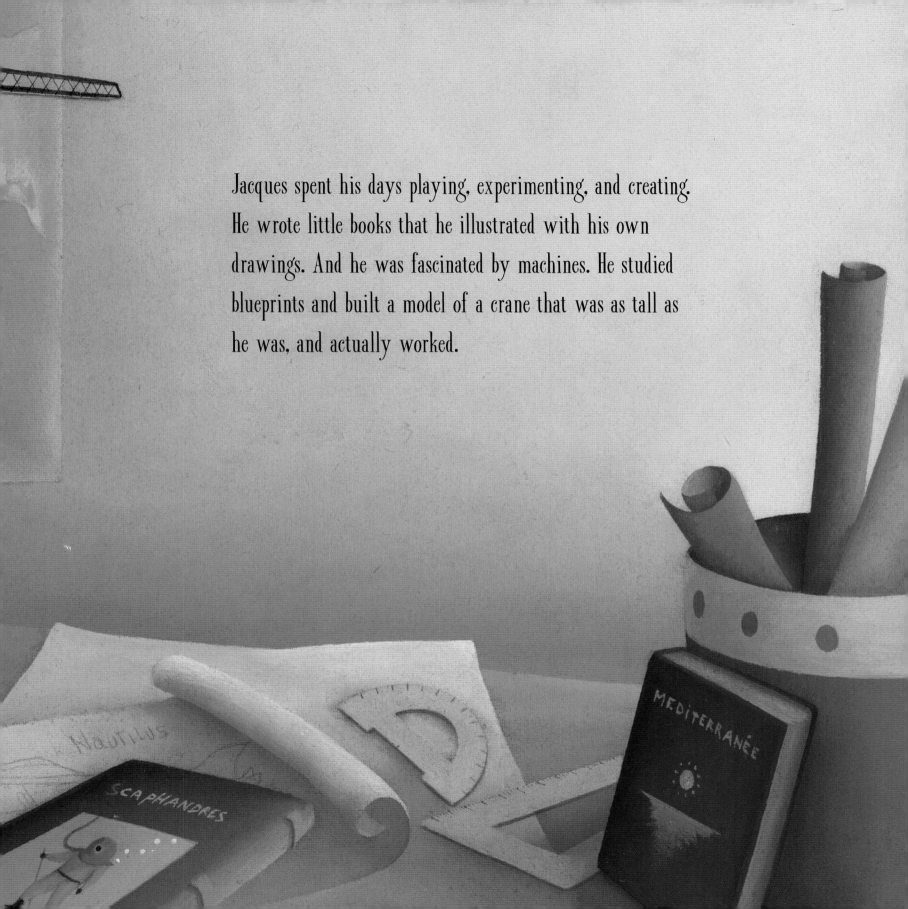

Jacques spent his days playing, experimenting, and creating.
He wrote little books that he illustrated with his own
drawings. And he was fascinated by machines. He studied
blueprints and built a model of a crane that was as tall as
he was, and actually worked.

Movies fascinated Jacques, too. He wanted to know how they were made, how the cameras worked, and how chemicals made pictures appear on the film. Jacques saved his allowance, penny by penny, until he had enough to buy a small home-movie camera. The first thing he did was take it apart and put it back together.

Then he began to film everything around him. He put his brother, cousins, parents, and friends in his movies. He dressed up as a villain with a painted-on mustache, and made some very villainous films. Jacques was always the star, the director, the writer. And usually the cameraman.

WHEN JACQUES FINISHED SCHOOL he joined
the French Navy. His ship sailed all around the world, and
everywhere he went he filmed what he saw.

In China, he filmed men catching fish with their bare hands.
They held their breath underwater for many minutes. Jacques
wondered what that would be like.

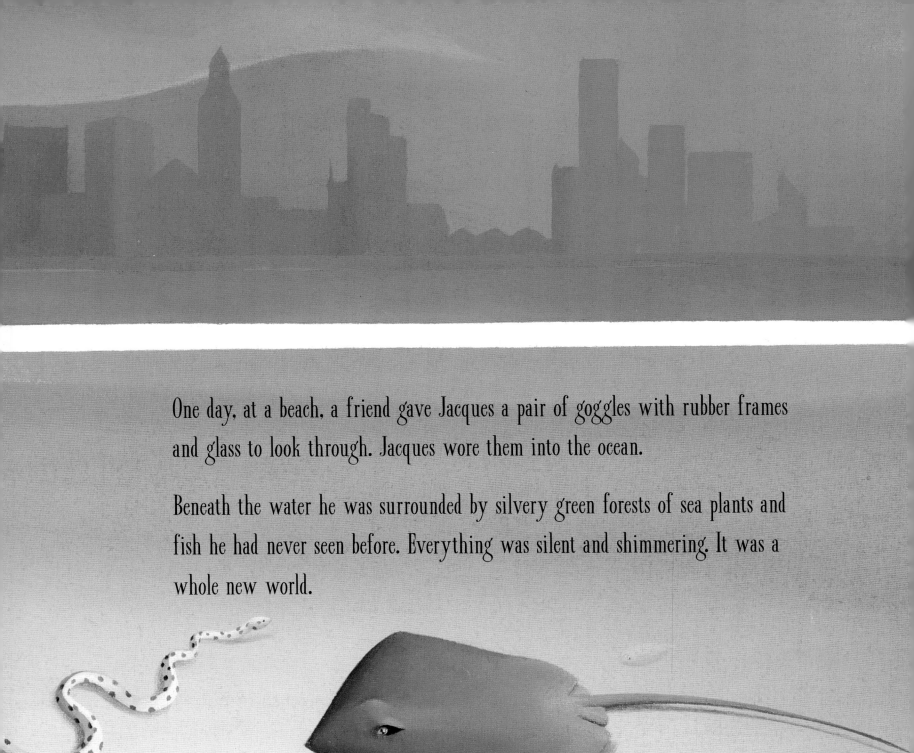

One day, at a beach, a friend gave Jacques a pair of goggles with rubber frames and glass to look through. Jacques wore them into the ocean.

Beneath the water he was surrounded by silvery green forests of sea plants and fish he had never seen before. Everything was silent and shimmering. It was a whole new world.

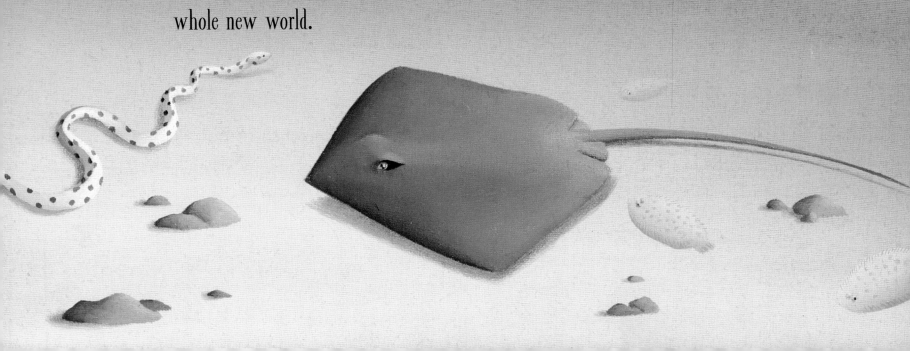

When he came up he saw cars, people, buildings, and telephone poles. Once again he went below into the magical underwater world. At that moment Jacques knew his life was changed forever. His eyes had been opened to the wonders of the sea.

Jacques and his friends, Philippe and Didi,
began to dive together. They experimented
to see how long they could stay underwater
and how deep they could go.

Jacques created a waterproof case for his
camera, to film the amazing kingdom he and his
friends were exploring beneath the surface.

They made rubber suits to keep themselves warm and flippers to help them kick better.

But Jacques wanted to stay down longer than just one breath at a time.

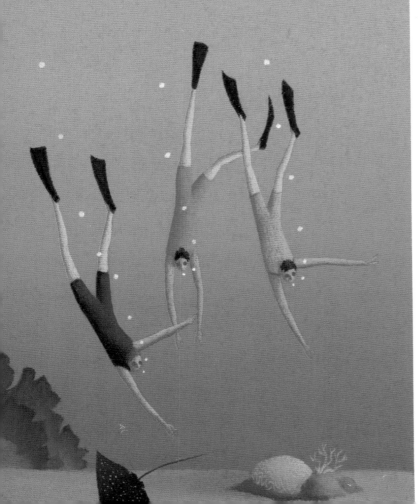

He realized he needed to take more air with him, enough air to explore the mysterious depths and vast expanses of the ocean. To swim through the sea as free as a fish.

He wanted to become a manfish.

And he began to work on just how to do it.

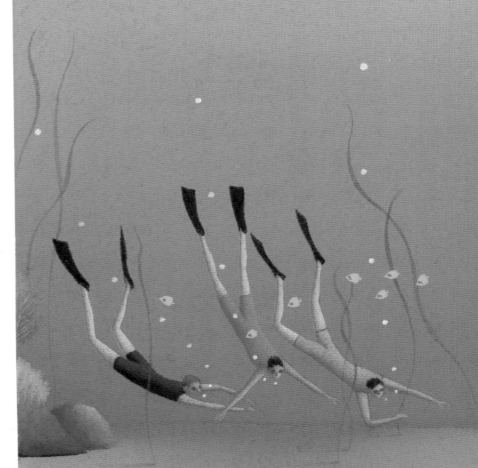

ON A WARM SUMMER DAY, Jacques stepped into the blue Mediterranean Sea with his new invention. He called it the aqualung—because *aqua* means water, and our lungs are the part of our body that holds the air we breathe.

Below the surface, Jacques swam and glided and dove. He did flips and somersaults.

He stood upside down on one finger, and laughed bubbles into the sea.

Jacques could breathe beneath the water!

Now he could swim across miles of ocean, his body feeling what only scales had felt, his eyes seeing what only fish had seen. The water made him feel like he was flying. Just like in his dreams.

Jacques had done it. He had become a manfish.

Jacques was ready to explore the oceans of the world. He needed a boat and found a big, old, wooden navy ship named *Calypso*. In a year he turned it from a warship into an explorer's ship.

Jacques, Philippe, and Didi gathered a crew, their aqualungs, their hopes, and their dreams, and set off to explore the inside of the sea, to film a world that no one had ever seen before.

On their journeys, they dove deep into a seascape of plants. Green and purple prickly plants. Red branchy plants. Spongy plants. Wispy, feathery, swaying plants, slow-dancing to the rhythms of the sea.

They discovered plants that could feed you. Plants that could poison you. Plants that looked like fish . . . and fish that looked like plants.

They swam with giant whales, hitched rides on sea turtles, and made friends with porpoises with shining eyes and smiling faces.

They filmed fierce and frightening sharks, so strange and dangerous Jacques and his crew had to build cages—not for the sharks, but for themselves—so they could make their movies without being eaten.

long fangs, lips like giant tires, and huge saucer eyes. They called it the truckfish.

On the bottom, they found pink ghost crabs, with eyes on long stalks, buried so deep in the sand they looked like a garden of eyes. And flute fish—with heads like horses and bodies the shape of tubes—sticking out of rocky openings, like pencils in a cup.

Their cameras captured camouflaged scorpion fish, ugly as
toads with poisonous spines. Dorados—brilliant,
fish that glowed the colors of emeralds,
sapphires, and rubies. Checkerboard fish, with
red and white checks from head to tail.

Deep down they discovered a kingdom of giant rays—fish
that fly through the water with wings that swim.

They came face to face with a fish as big as a truck—with

Everywhere the *Calypso* went, Jacques and his crew made films of what they saw. Films that played in movie theaters. Films that played on TV.

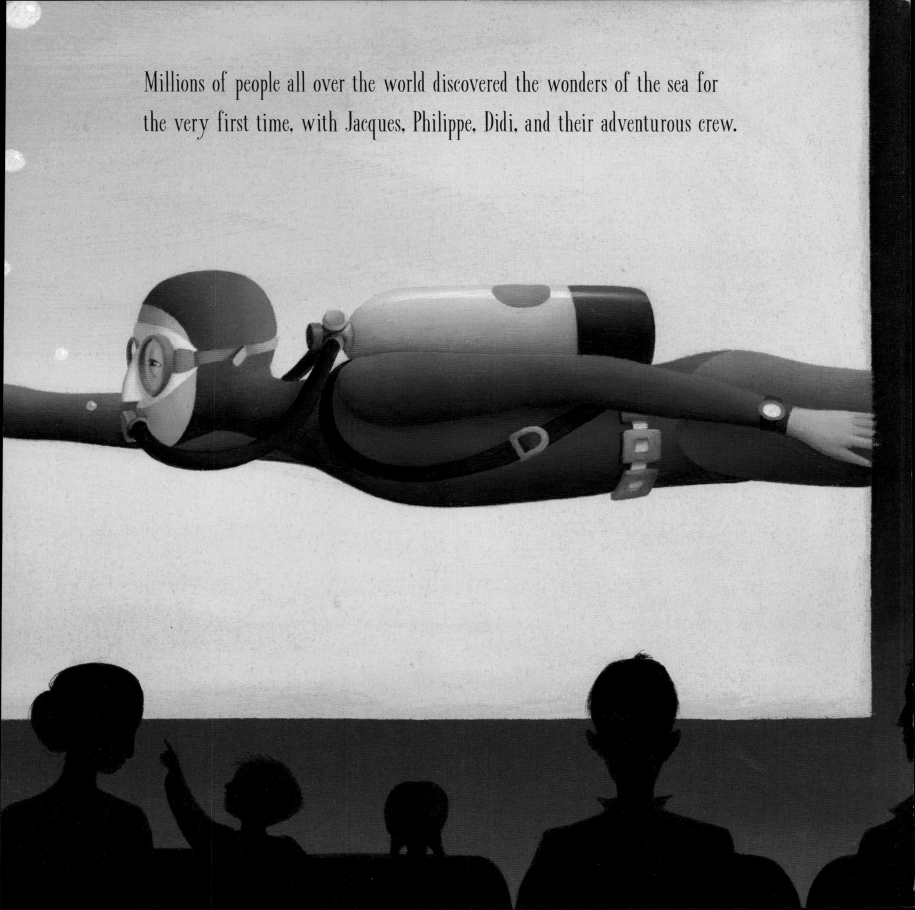

Millions of people all over the world discovered the wonders of the sea for the very first time, with Jacques, Philippe, Didi, and their adventurous crew.

After Jacques spent most of his life making movies about the
sea, he saw something happening. Something shocking.

Plants that used to be alive and healthy were being poisoned.
Fish were sick and dying.

Jacques saw that people, without realizing it, were slowly killing the sea and its creatures, by dumping garbage and poisonous chemicals into the ocean he loved so much.

Jacques knew what he had to do. He had to make movies. Movies to warn people. Movies to save the sea.

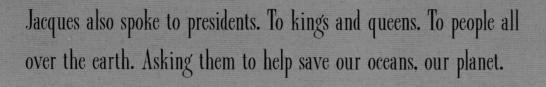

Jacques also spoke to presidents. To kings and queens. To people all over the earth. Asking them to help save our oceans, our planet.

And he spoke to children.

Jacques dreamed that someday it would be you, exploring worlds never seen, never imagined. Whole new worlds, silent and shimmering. Worlds that are now yours. To discover. To care for. And to love.

Author's Note

Jacques Cousteau was a remarkable person, truly one-of-a-kind. He was a protector of our planet and its creatures, an inventor, adventurer and explorer, a poetic writer and spokesperson for the sea. He was also an innovative filmmaker and photographer. Most of all, he loved life with a childlike sense of joy and an insatiable curiosity.

His rallying cry wherever he went, whatever he was exploring, was "Il faut aller voir," which translates roughly as "We must go and see for ourselves," which I think is a wonderful way to start just about anything. I feel fortunate for all the time I spent in Jacques Cousteau's world while researching and writing this book.

If you'd like some more Cousteau in your life, here are a few ideas:

JOIN: The Cousteau Society (www.cousteau.org), founded by Jacques Cousteau in 1973 for research, exploration, and education. Join as a "Cousteau Kid," to receive *Cousteau Kids* magazine every other month.

COUSTEAU'S FILMS: Jacques Cousteau made over 115 films. Some are available now from your library or for sale over the Internet, and thanks to the Cousteau Society, almost all of them will be available on DVD by 2009.

COUSTEAU'S BOOKS: Cousteau wrote over 50 books, full of beautiful pictures and fascinating adventures. Just recently, his important last book, *The Human, The Orchid, and the Octopus,* was released in the United States.

THE MARINE WORLD: Most natural history museums have wonderful, informative exhibits about the ocean world. You can also visit ocean research centers or take snorkeling or diving lessons.

CARING FOR OUR PLANET: Cousteau believed that each of us has a responsibility to protect the earth. You can do your part every single day by turning off the water while brushing your teeth, encouraging your family to walk more and ride their bikes, and by turning off the lights when you leave a room. Making an effort to recycle helps, too.

FOLLOWING COUSTEAU'S LEAD: Get a camera and start photographing or filming what interests you. Motivate your family and friends to start caring about the world and its creatures. Above all (I'm sure Cousteau would agree with this): follow your passions, follow your dreams.

J. B.